Nakajima Ki.84 a/b HAYATE

In Japanese Army Air Force Service

Richard M. Bueschel

Schiffer Military/Aviation History
Atglen, PA

Cover artwork by Steve Ferguson, Colorado Springs, CO

WHEN THE STORM DIES—In the summer of 1944, Major Iwashi took command of the newly designated 22nd Sentai, the elite regiment which would take their superb new Nakajima Ki.84 HAYATE (Hurricane) into the new offensive in central China. So stunning was Iwashi's success, his unit would be one of only four Army flying units, and the sole fighter regiment to be permitted use of the royal sacred crhrysanthemum for their personal insignia.

However, the honor was all too fleeting. As of late September, Iwashi's regiment transitioned from the tenuous offensive in China to the fateful defense of the Phillippine Islands. The American invasion was spearheaded by a well trained, well equipped carrier air wing storming over the Marianna Islands and central Phillippines in far more numbers than ever encountered to date. Despite an influx of JAAF Hayate units joining the 22nd Regiment in the great battle, they were quickly overwhelmed. After the fall of the Phillippines and subsequent full retreat to the home islands, the last of the venerable Hayates would languish in reserve for the final invasion which would never be.

Acknowledgments
Thanks are due to the photo sources cited, with special thanks to Richard L. Seely of Aero Literature for permission to reproduce the photographs from the R. L. Seely Collection; James F. Lansdale for proofing and editing of the original edition for historical accuracy, and James I. Long for bringing the text up to date with current practice nomenclature, model and unit identification.

This title was originally published by Osprey Publications Ltd. in 1970.

Book Design by Ian Robertson.

Printed in China.
ISBN: 0-7643-0149-7

We are interested in hearing from authors with book ideas on related topics.

Published by Schiffer Publishing Ltd.
77 Lower Valley Road
Atglen, PA 19310
Phone: (610) 593-1777
FAX: (610) 593-2002
E-mail: schifferbk@aol.com
Please write for a free catalog.
This book may be purchased from the publisher.
Please include $2.95 postage.
Try your bookstore first.

Prototype Ki.84 serial 8401 was completed in March 1943 and test flown in April. Single exhaust stack is characteristic of first three experimental models only. M. Toda.

NAKAJIMA Ki.84 Hayate

As the American transport vessels and their escorts headed north toward Luzon from Panay Island in the center of the Philippines, they were covered by a protective screen of carrier-based F4U Corsairs. USAAF land-based P-38 Lightnings were also on hand, ranging over the Mindoro Straits from their bases on Leyte. The lookouts on board ship began to relax. The day was coming to an end as the sun sank lower toward the sea to the west. The date was 5 January 1945, and the possibility of attack from the air was negligible as the Japanese air forces in the Philippines had been all but destroyed. One month earlier, on 7 December, the

Americans had blasted a reported 56 Japanese planes out of the skies over Leyte for the loss of a single P-38 Lightning. Since that date Japanese attacks from the air had been sporadic, with suicide attacks largely replacing conventional raids.

Suddenly, out of the north, five bomb-laden Japanese fighters appeared at an altitude of about 6,000 feet to begin their dive and skip-bombing runs on the transport ships. With over a hundred vessels in the convoy, the waters were filled with targets of opportunity. Just as quickly, the Corsairs closed in on the fighters as a massive screen of anti-aircraft fire filled the sky with bursts of slash-

Second experimental Ki.84 serial 8402 was completed in June 1943. Tail markings are "02" taken from last two digits of serial number 8402. After new camouflage paint scheme had been applied the number was changed to "102" which appears as the "1" dash above the "02" on the fin and as a yellow stencil serial "102" barely visible just forward and below the stabilizer leading edge. M. Toda

ing shrapnel. Coming up from the southeast, some 32 American Army P-38's began to climb to intercept the intruders. Everything was happening at once !

Moving themselves into a tight attack formation, the Japanese pilots closed their cockpit canopies, set their tabs full down, and dived into the wall of flak. Cutting off the defending American fighters with the brutal firing from below, they headed for the largest troop transports at the rear of the convoy. Lopsided from their single 550-pound bombs suspended from one wing, originally balanced by an auxiliary fuel tank that had been dropped prior to the attack, the radial powered Japanese planes came in at an angle of about 60 degrees. One burst into flames, then exploded and began spewing chunks of aircraft all over the sky. Another, by now hitting an indicated air speed of over 450 m.p.h., took a hit at the back of the canopy just as it dropped its bomb. Then the rest of the canopy came of, and the pilot was all but pulled out of the cockpit by air pressure. Miraculously, he levelled out the fighter

Second experimental aircraft serial 8402 tested the suitability of the Ho.3 wing mounted 20mm cannon and fuselage mounts for the Ho.5 20mm cannon. Central drop tank fitting under fuselage. M. Toda.

The second experimental Ki.84 entered the service testing program at Fussa Flight Test Center in August 1943. It was learned that the single exhaust stack did not make use of exhaust gasses for thrust, so the system was reengineered. M. Toda.

barely above the waterline, and below the deck level of the transport he had just hit in the stern with a high-explosive bomb.

Spotted by those on deck as a "Frank", the newest Japanese Army fighter to see service in the Philippines, the topless attacker threaded its way through the crowded convoy at over 300 m.p.h. Just as it began to pull out of its predicament it took a hit on its hydraulic system. The right landing gear started to drop, braking the aircraft's speed like a sledge hammer, as the "Frank" disappeared into a cloud of black smoke. The convoy had just seen the new Japanese Army Air Force (JAAF) Ki.84 Type 4 Fighter in action, the latest of a long line of single-seat radial-engined fighters built by Nakajima. The result of a direct line of development, the Ki.84 was an advanced descendent of the Ki.27 97 Sen, Ki.43 Hayabusa and Ki.44 Shoki series of fighters produced by the same manufacturer. Known as the Hayate to the Japanese Army, in translation the Hurricane, the new fighter was easily the equal of its opponents, and superior in per-

formance to many of the American and British fighters it met in combat.

Shaken by his experience, with his head in the open air and his right landing gear hanging one-third down, Captain Shiro Kono of the 1st Air Regiment looked back at the holocaust below as his Hayate broke clear after blindly flying through a

Single drop tank was revealed to be inadequate for long-range offensive missions. Sekai no Kokuki.

Wing racks were tested on pre-production models to develop universal racks to hold 30kg. to 250kg. bombs as well as fuel drop tanks. Koku Fan.

Action over Luzon in the Philippines. A Ki.84A Hayate takes off with a bomb on its right wing and a drop tank on the left. Hideya Ando.

dome of black smoke and pulled away from the scene of battle. Bursting out of the flak screen, he was attacked by four American F4U Corsair fighters that had been waiting overhead. Evading his foes to the best of his ability as the sky darkened, Kono was soon left alone as the Corsairs gave up

Large oil cooler was characteristic of Type 4 Fighter Ki.84 production models. Sekai no Kokuki.

in disgust. Heading home in the dark, with an hour of flying time ahead of him, the army air force captain reflected on the overwhelming strength of the enemy and the hopelessness of Japan's position. Finally reaching his home base on Southern Luzon, Kono's Hayate was joined by only one other. Three 1st Air Regiment pilots had died in the battle, flying fighters as dive-bombers, unable to defend themselves. Four days later the American 6th Army began its massive Luzon landings to the north at Lingayen Gulf, and by the end of the month Philippines skies were under complete control of Allied airpower. Beaten and grounded, the Japanese air forces were either decimated or in retreat. The Philippines campaign was over and all that was left was the cleaning-up. The aircraft losses were to leave Japan almost defenseless, and the Japanese Army's best fighters had been thrown away by the hundreds as most of the Hayate production to date was lost in the campaign.

But the Hayate had made its mark. It would be met again in quantity over Okinawa, Japan, China and Manchukuo. Nakajima's final fighter was ready for the final fight. It was soon in coming.

Beginning The End of the Line

It is said that the moment any aircraft reaches production it is obsolete. By the time a fighter has been tested and tooled, and starts to come off the line to enter service, its designers have already gone well beyond it in their minds and are thinking about what they can do next to make an even better aircraft. With the Ki.43 Hayabusa just beginning to enter service as the Pacific War began, both the JAAF

Newest Army fighter in service, the Ki.84A was rushed into combat with many existing units re-equipped with the fighter in the summer of 1944. Koku Shonen.

and Nakajima management began to consider the next generation fighter. The Army wanted an all-purpose penetration fighter that combined the handling characteristics of the nimble Ki.43 with the performance of the heavier Ki.44 Shoki that was also technologically simplified. It took 25,000 man hours to produce a Hayabusa, and even though it was smaller, the Shoki still required 24,000 man hours. No matter how the new war progressed, the Japanese Army knew that its fighter demand requirements would increase. One way to get more

fighters was to cut the production time in half, if that was possible, in turn providing twice as many aircraft in the same time period utilizing existing manufacturing facilities. On 29 December 1941, exactly three weeks after Japan went to war with the ABD powers (American, British and Dutch), the JAAF gave Nakajima the specifications for the new fighter. One of the most exciting features of the new requirements was the specified use of the Nakajima Ha.45 engine, a new 2,000 h.p. radial that was just being developed by the firm. Tei Koyama, freed from

The brittle landing gear legs and the unreliable Homare engine of the Hayate led to high non-combat losses in the Philippines. Hal Andrews.

A new Hayate of the 2nd Company, 73rd Fighter Air Regiment, arrives in the Philippines in December 1944. Daily Asahi.

the long-term demands of the Ki.44 Shoki (which was now on operational test and would enter mass production in a matter of months) became the chief project engineer. By April 1942 rough thoughts on a fighter that could be produced in an estimated 14,000 man hours were reviewed with the Army. On 27 May 1942 Nakajima received an order from the JAAF for the Ki.84 Army Experimental Heavy Fighter, and preliminary work began.

Few World War II high-performance fighters were developed so fast. By March 1943, only ten months later, the prototype serial 8401, was completed, and in less than five weeks it made its first

Hayates of the 73rd Air Regiment were both natural dural (2nd Company aircraft at left) and drab camouflaged (1st Company aircraft at right rear) in Philippines service. Sekai no Kokuki.

Aircraft No.91 in red markings of 2nd Company, 73rd Air Regiment, is natural dural which led to confusion with American fighters over Luzon. Maru.

Individual aircraft marking of 73rd Air Regiment is based on aircraft factory number. This Hayate is production number 491, with last two digits used as 2nd Company identification as "91". Koku Asahi.

Hayate aircraft "66" in white tail markings of 1st Company, 73rd Air Regiment. Three digit factory number is unknown, but ends in "66." White combat stripe is carryover from earlier Ki.43 Hayabusa days and was soon dropped. USN.

Ki.84A of the 1st Company, 73rd Fighter Air Regiment, on Luzon, December 1944. Spinner is white in company color. Koku Shonen.

高速を誇

2nd Company Ki.84A Hayate, 73rd Air Regiment, with red tail stripes and spinner. Hiko Shonen.

flight at Ojima Airfield in April. The Army Air Test Department at Fussa was under great pressure to evaluate the aircraft as rapidly as possible, for the tide of war had turned. Far to the south, in New Guinea, the JAAF 4th Air Army was feeling the pressure of the Allied air forces, losing hundreds of its aircraft without any major accomplishments. The Army was running out of fighters, and the new Ki.84 was desperately needed to counter the new Allied aircraft making their appearance. In June 1943 the

prototype made an appearance at the Akeno Fighter Army Flying School, flown in by Fussa test pilot Major Iwabashi, where it dazzled instructors and students alike. Iwabashi explained that the new fighter was so simple to fly, that unskilled pilots with only 200 hours in the air could handle it. To prove it, Iwabashi made repeated demonstration flights, making landings in about a thousand feet and using up only two-thirds of the Akeno runway. It was a master public relations stroke, for the personnel

新鋭單座戰

Ki.84A mounted 2 x 12.7mm Ho.103 guns in nose and a 20mm Ho.5 cannon in each wing. Asahigraph.

In attempts to improve engine reliability Homare Ha.45 Models 11, 12, 21 and 23 were progressively mounted on the Ki.84A.

Ki.84A and subsequent production models featured individual jet type exhaust stacks which added thrust and broke up the exhaust flame pattern into smaller, less visible points of light at night. Koku Asahi.

at the JAAF's top fighter school could hardly wait for the new mount. With the Kawasaki Ki.61-I Hien just entering service, and the Ki.84 coming soon, morale throughout Army Air was boosted at a critical time.

June was also the month the second experimental model, serial 8102, was completed. Incorporating numerous changes based on experience with 8401, it was flying in August. A third experimental aircraft serial 8403 quickly followed. Look-

ing much like overgrown Hayabusas, the three test aircraft had single large exhausts and center line fittings for a single drop tank or bomb. Hitting 624 km./hr. (388 m.p.h.) the new fighters were faster than their predecessors, but still below the hoped-for performance. But the production advantages were enormous. The switch to the Ki.84 at Nakajima's Ota plant production lines could be made so quickly and easily it would hardly be noticed. Koyama, by now a director of the company,

More Hayates were destroyed on the ground than in the air in the Philippines. Koku Shonen.

The Philippines campaign provided invading American forces with numerous examples of the new Type 4 Fighter. Hayate losses in the Philippines literally drained the JAAF of all Type 4 Fighter production in 1944. Koku Fan.

A surfeit of captured examples of the Ki.84A led to the destruction of needless Hayates that had suffered from aerial attack. Here a Hayate gets the torch at Luzon. Jack Canary.

had designed his aircraft to make use of the same jigs then being used to produce the Ki.43 Hayabusa. Another production development was the adoption of the Kijunko Shuseiho (standardized drilling collection) system, a method of drilling from patterns that eliminated hand measurements, thereby increasing accuracy while speeding up the work.

The Bird Leaves The Nest

With testing of the first three experimental aircraft proceeding, the Army ordered Nakajima to rush right into construction of a batch of improved models for service evaluation prior to production approval. Engineering improvements had been started as soon as the prototype serial 8401 was in the air, and by

Miraculously intact, a Ki.84A Hayate of the 2nd Company, 11th Fighter Air Regiment is discovered by Americans at Clark Field, January 28, 1945. USAAF.

Company markings of aircraft "46," 2nd Company, 11th Air Regiment, are red edged in white over a drab finish. Individual aircraft number is white. USAAF.

August 1943 the first of the pre-production models had been completed. The exhaust system now had separate thrust-augmented stacks, and racks were added to each wing to allow the aircraft to carry two tanks or 250 kg. bombs, or one of each. Rushed over to Fussa in September 1943, the new model was flown in mock combat with its brother Ki.44 Shoki as well as one of the JAAF's proudest possessions, a German Focke-Wulf Fw.190 A/5 that had arrived in Japan earlier that summer. Test pilot Major Yasuhiki Kuroe, a former Shoki combat pilot now assigned to Fussa, rated the Nakajima Ki.84 higher than both competitive aircraft in maneuverability, but reported with some concern that the German fighter decidedly had the advantage in speed and dive tests.

Between August and March 1944 a total of 83 evaluation models were produced, with testing of

The spoils of war! Type 3 Fighter Hien in foreground, Type 4 Fighter Hayate in background at left, Philippines. Koku Fan.

Code named "Frank," the Hayates found at Clark Field immediately came under Technical Air Intelligence Unit control for evaluation. Badly damaged examples were bulldozed or burned. USN.

various attributes starting as soon as examples were available. As the tests progressed, the airframes on the production line were modified based on experience, in effect working out production problems as the performance was enhanced. Step by step the fuselage underwent evolutionary changes as the tail configuration was being finalized to overcome a torque problem. By October 1943 a flight training company had been formed at Akeno to test the Ki.84's performance in an actual unit. Over the winter the experimental group ironed out the organizational bugs faced with the new fighter. By March 1944, in accordance with JAAF practice, the training unit was disbanded, with most of the pilots being transferred to the newly-formed Fussa-based 22nd Air Regiment, the first combat unit to receive the fighter. Under command of Major Iwashi, the 22nd Air Regiment started its unit training with preproduction models powered by the Ha.45/11. A second batch of evaluation models

A prize of war! Superior condition Ki.84A Hayate of 1st Company, 1st Fighter Air regiment captured on Luzon. USN.

Out comes the measuring tape. Finding an intact "Frank" was more than air intelligence could have hoped for. Lines are marking tapes to measure dimensions. Red rudder denotes 1st Company, 1st Air Regiment. USN.

were started in the same month, with 42 being completed by June. In April, the Army authorized mass production as the Type 4 Fighter, Model A, Ki.84A, and named it Hayate. With evaluation and Type 4 service models being produced on parallel lines, the availability of the fighter jumped as Hayabusa production ended. By June monthly production topped 100 aircraft, and by October the monthly rate was over 300.

Broad acceptance by the JAAF of the Hayate as the Hayabusa's replacement put the spotlight on the 22nd Air Regiment. With over 20 existing regiments scheduled for the Hayate, and half as many new Ki.84 regiments yet to be formed, the

Taking the measure of the enemy with more tape. Dimensional tapes wrap half way around the spinner and down one prop blade. This aircraft was later the subject of intensive flight testing. USN.

First operational photograph of the Type 4 Fighter Hayate appeared in the Japanese press in January 1945. The aircraft was unidentified. Koku Asahi.

Meet The Press: The Hayate is displayed for the Japanese press, April 1945. Koku Asahi.

maintenance and performance of the fighter was of critical importance. Skilled crews kept the various pre-production and Ki.84A production models of Hayate in top shape as pilots and potential unit commanders rotated through the 22nd Regiment. The results were almost bugless, and the Hayate was on its way to war as almost the most perfect new fighter to enter JAAF service. This reliance on perfection, particularly the "tender-loving-care" given to the sophisticated Ha.45/11 engines, was later to cost the JAAF dearly, for the Hayate was being measured for combat under controlled con-

Meet The Press: The Japanese press was eager to show off the new Army defense weapon to protect Japanese skies, except the Hayate couldn't do the job very well. From the front, April 1945. Koku Asahi.

Meet The Press: The Japanese press agencies had wide contacts throughout the Greater East-Asia Co-Prosperity Sphere to impress the populace with the Hayate. From the rear, April 1945. Koku Asahi.

Meet the Press: The press introduction of the Hayate was neutered, with unit markings retouched out. Three-quarter front, April 1945. Koku Asahi.

Hayates of the 1st Company, 102nd Fighter Air Regiment, take off on a mission against American fighters over Okinawa, May 1945. Hideya Ando.

ditions. In actual combat the survivability factor would prove to be far different.

By the middle of the summer the unit was ready to face the enemy, and 30 or so production Ki.84A Hayates of the 22nd Air Regiment were shipped over to Hankow, China, where they joined the Shoki equipped 85th Air Regiment. Pitted against the USAAF Mustangs and Lightnings of General Chennault's 14th Air Force, the Hayates first met the enemy late in August. The results were electrifying. Expecting the slower JAAF fighters they had become accustomed to, the Americans suddenly found themselves faced with a tougher adversary.

Formed of crack pilots transferred from other JAAF regiments, the 22nd was soon in command of the sky over its domain, and quickly put the JAAF back on the offensive.

The Crunch of Combat

Back in Japan, Hayate unit formation got under way rapidly. By the end of September the 1st, 11th, 21st, 51st, 52nd, 70th, 71st, 85th, 103rd and 246th Air Regiments had received the fighter. New regiments, outgrowths of the 1st, 8th, 10th, 13th and 14th Flight Drilling Units, were also being established, with the Hayate, on its way to becoming the most widely-

New Hayate units were formed as existing units were decimated. Maru.

As the war inched closer and closer to Japan, Hayates were retained for Home Island Defense. Sekai no Kokuki.

Allied fighters over Japan, and a Hayate goes to meet them. N. Saito.

The lonely warrior, a Ki.84A Hayate waits for the whistle to blow, late April 1945. Koku Asahi.

used fighter in the JAAF in the last year of the war. The rapidity of the build-up was directly related to enemy successes in the Pacific, for the decisive battles of the war were coming closer to reality. Anticipating major Allied assaults against the Philippines or Formosa by September 1944, or even Japan by November, an Army-Navy Central Agreement was worked out so that their combined air forces could be concentrated at the point of battle. Growing pressure on the Philippines, and a sudden acceleration of Allied air strikes, ultimately led Imperial General Headquarters to the correct conclusion that a Philippines invasion was only weeks away. Plans for Sho Operation No. 1, code name for the Philippines battle to end the war in Japan's favor, were underway. The 51st and 52nd Hayate Air Regiments were ordered to the Philippines with the 16th Air Brigade. The 22nd Air Regiment, in China for only five weeks, was pulled out and joined the 1st and 11th Air Regiments of the 12th Air Brigade where they were assigned to the Clark Field area and lower Luzon. On 11 October, the new 200th Air Regiment was also assigned to the Philippines, with unit formation at Akeno beginning the next day. All of the units came under the command of the 30th Fighter Group, exclusively equipped with

Defender of Japan, the Hayate was incapable of meeting the American B-29 Superfortress at altitude. An upward cannon firing model was envisioned as the Ki.84D. Sekai no Kokuki.

A rare sight. A home defense Hayate sits out in the open surrounded by a quick camouflage fix of loose mats. Koku Fan.

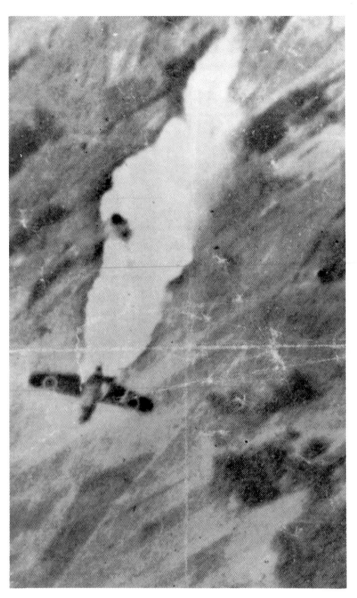

A "Frank" is downed by a USAAF Mustang over Tokyo. USAAF.

the Hayate. A final October addition was the 24th Independent Air Company, a former Hayabusa unit re-equipped with the Hayate.

The new strength arrived just in time. The available Hayate units found themselves fighting for their lives when, on 14 and 15 October, Allied carrier fighters came over by the hundreds. Then, on 17 October, the American invasion of the Philippines began with a massive landing at Leyte. At that moment all of the plans for Sho Operation No. 1 were activated. The Hayates of the 30th Fighter Group went into action as dive and skip bombers from their Central Philippines' forward bases to attack enemy invasion ships off Leyte. Some 70 Hayates were on hand for the missions, with more on the way from Japan as reinforcements as the newly-produced fighters were rushed into service. With the arrival of the 200th Air Regiment on 25 and 26 October, the 4th Air Army was theoretically ready for the co-ordinated air offensive scheduled to halt the invasion. Almost 400 Army and Navy aircraft were prepared for the battle, with the odds in their favor as they outnumbered their enemy in the air over their own ground.

The battle actually began on 24 October when 80 JAAF aircraft were thrown against the American landing ships, followed by 38 in the afternoon, and another 29 at dusk. As the days passed, the efficiency of the Hayate units dropped rapidly. The optimum maintenance conditions experienced in Japan and China did not exist in the Philippines, and mechanical difficulties that had never been

Make-shift maintenance kept as many of the touchy Hayates in the air as possible. M. Toda.

Red tipped vertical tail denotes 2nd Battalion, 111th Fighter Air Regiment, Central Defense Sector, Japan. 1st Battalion had similar markings in white. N. Saito.

anticipated began to show up in profusion. The Ha.45/11 and Ha.45/12 engines of the Ki.84A model proved to be almost totally unreliable under field maintenance conditions. Flying aircraft they had only recently acquired, many Hayate pilots found the powerful aircraft getting away from them. Propeller wake, hitting the dropped landing flaps, often snapped the aircraft's nose down, and only a skilled pilot could prevent an accident. Many didn't,

Late production Ki.84A of 2nd Battalion, 111th Fighter Air Regiment, Gifu, Japan, July 1945. N. Saito.

and the aircraft were washed out. Landing itself was always a minor miracle, for the metallurgy of the landing gear legs depreciated as production rates increased. Poor heat-treating made the main members so brittle that the Hayate pilots often cynically joked about the "4-Sen's easy breaking legs". If the landing wasn't just perfect, the legs would snap, with the pilot skidding in at 100 m.p.h. completely out of control. It even happened if the tire pressure was a little too high. The landing gear couldn't take the shock. The replacement parts, when they were available, were just as bad. On one delivery flight 80 Hayates started out from Japan on 4 November. Only 14 of them reached their destination at Lingayen Gulf, with the other 66 lost en route or dropping out due to engine trouble, landing gear failures, or fuel system and hydraulic problems.

Replacement aircraft received from Japan had consistently lower top speeds than the previous batch. Rated at over 600 km./hr. when the Hayate was introduced, by the end of 1944 only the rare Ki.84A could reach a speed of 400 km./hr. Climb rates and service ceilings also suffered, with pilots

A combat weary Hayate of the 111th Air Regiment awaits the next alert over the Central Defense Sector, July 1945. N. Saito.

drawing straws to get a "good" Hayate instead of one of the "lemons" delivered to the combat units.

In spite of its deficiencies, in the hands of a skilled pilot the Hayate was a worthy foe. It handled well in the air, and once a pilot mastered its idiosyncrasies his chances of survival and combat success were on a par with the enemy. Facing a determined foe flying advanced aircraft, the American invaders of Leyte recognized the immediate need for land-based fighters to protect the landing operations. On 27 October, immediately after acquisition of the airfield at Tacloban, the USAAF 5th Air Force moved in with P-38 Lightnings. 33 of them were flying from the field the first day, with over 60 by the end of the month. They quickly established local air superiority, squaring off with the Hayate units in daily battles. The handwriting was on the wall.

Losing the Philippines

The aggressive attacks of the dive-bombing Hayates barely made a dent in the invasion forces. Losing ground day-by-day, the 4th Air Army called for more reinforcements. Eleven new fighter and

Coming in the hard way, but still in one piece. Hayate of the 520th Temporary Interception Regiment skidded in to a relatively undamaged landing with all four prop blades hitting. Sekai no Kokuki.

Tokyo air defense Hayate "46" with red tail marks of 2nd Company, 47th Fighter Air Regiment. Robert C. Mikesh.

bomber regiments were readied for the Philippines. Equipped with Hayates, the 29th and 246th Air Regiments arrived in mid-November, with the quickly formed 71st Air Regiment landing at the end of the month, followed by the 72nd and 73rd Air Regiments early in December. They were accompanied by the loud fanfare of the Japanese Press. Reaching the battle front at a time when American air strength was climbing in geometric progression,

the Hayate units were quickly chewed up. Within a few weeks the 73rd Air Regiment was wiped out, to be quietly disbanded on paper in the official records in Tokyo the following May. The Philippines campaign rapidly took on the aspects of a disaster as JAAF losses, running at 52 per cent of strength in October, jumped to 79 per cent by the third week of November. Most of these losses were non-combative, with the majority of the aircraft lost on the

Wreckage on the repair rack. Koku Fan.

Hayates ready for suicidal "Body Crashing" sorties against Allied shipping around Okinawa. Sekai no Kokuki.

Taking off on a special attack suicide mission against Allied forces around Okinawa in a bomb laden Hayate. Sekai no Kokuki.

Smashed home defense Hayate with red wingtips at Kiru, Japan, August 1945. Holmes G. Anderson.

ground. In an attempt to realign its forces to reverse the trend, the 4th Air Army shuffled unit assignments with the 2nd Air Army to the south to better prepare itself for further invasion attempts. By 8 December, the 4th Air Army had only 133 operational aircraft left. And the worst was yet to come. On 7 December, this strength was cut almost in half in air battles over Leyte. The final invasion at Lingayen Gulf was only a month away.

The JAAF pilots that survived the Philippines campaign often felt they lived charmed lives. Major Ikida Takano, Commander of the 52nd Air Regiment, survived the campaign and the war, as did Major Saburo Togo, Commander of the 1st Air Regiment. Togo ranked as an ace with 21 "kills" of Allied aircraft. Other scoring Hayate survivors were Warrant Officer Katsuaki Kira, who went on to the

Industrial defense, with Hayate of the 1st Company, 104th Fighter Air Regiment at Anzan, Manchukuo, in the foreground after the successful Soviet invasion of August 1945. Second aircraft is Tachikawa Ki.55 trainer, with more Hayates in the background. Robert C. Mikesh.

Burned out Ki.84A Hayates at Kiru, Japan, at the end of the war. Red wingtips are home defense markings. Holmes G. Anderson.

Okinawan campaign and ended the war with 25 "kills"; Captain Shiro Kono of the 1st Regiment; Eisuke Tsusake of the 72nd Air Regiment; and many others who flew or scampered out of the Philippines ahead of the advancing Americans.

Others were not so lucky and the losses were enormous. Major Toshio Sakagawa, commander of the 200th Air Regiment, and one of the few JAAF pilots to almost reach the half-century mark as an ace, was shot down over Leyte. He had 49 "kills" to his credit. Bombed on the ground, shot out of the sky, and continually threatened by mechanical failures, the Hayate pilot was a man on the spot. But the battle was not always one-sided. On 24 December, returning from the interception of B-24 Liberators attacking Clark Field, a 1st Air Regiment pilot was jumped at low altitude by four P-38's over his base when his fuel was all but gone. While the ground crewmen below cheered, the five aircraft above tangled in full view. A veteran of four years of combat with over 2,000 flying hours behind him, the Hayate pilot held his fire while the Lightnings

continued to attack him one at a time. Suddenly climbing, he downed two P-38's in one climbing pass. The other two Lightnings quickly departed as the Hayate turned to land with empty fuel tanks.

One Hayate of the 1st Air Regiment had to be discarded when its pilot dived out of an ambush by sixteen American Navy Hellcats at 20,000 feet. Coming straight down, and hitting almost 500

Curious American inspects Ki.84A "Frank" in a defeated Japan. In the background are Nakajima-built G3M3 96 Rikko "Nell" JNAF bombers fitted with MAD sub detection gear ready to be burned or bulldozed into the water. Koku Fan.

Hayate wreckage littered the Japanese countryside on the airfields surrounding Japan's major cities. Sekai no Kokuki.

Junk piles of Hayates and other aircraft were soon burned and removed by Japanese military working under instructions of the Allied occupation forces. Sekai no Kokuki.

m.p.h., the pilot barely pulled it out and got back home. The dural skin was so wrinkled, and so many rivets had popped, the aircraft was completely useless. On another occasion, flying back to Clark Field at low altitude from a dive-bombing mission two days before the Lingayen Gulf invasion, a Hayate pilot ran into four Grumman Hellcats on the prowl. With a damaged landing gear hanging down serving to tempt the American fighters into battle, the Japanese pilot pushed the aircraft into a valley at treetop height to get away. One Hellcat followed. Misjudging the speed, the American plane overran its target, and was immediately shot down. To avenge their buddy, the other Hellcats closed in, just as the Hayate headed toward a low mountain. Suddenly, the Hayate dropped its combat flaps and made a tight turn to the left. The lead Hellcat, caught

in the trap, flipped to the right but couldn't clear the trees. It exploded in the hillside. The Hayate escaped as the other two Hellcats recovered control, with nothing left to do but return to their carrier.

By the end of January the campaign was over. When American forces took over Clark Field on 28 January 1945, Japanese air activity was brought to an end. As a reminder of the confrontations of the past three months, the new masters of Luzon found numerous examples of the Hayate in the area, with some in almost mint condition. Immediately placed in the hands of the Technical Air Intelligence Unit —South-west Pacific Area (TAIU-SWPA), the friendly "Frank" was refurbished and test flown. Evaluation would reveal the aircraft's good points, and pinpoint the bad, so that Allied pilots would have first-hand knowledge of what they

Hayate Ki.84-II with wooden components in Southern Japan, ready for the Allied invasion scheduled for November 1945. Millions of lives, mostly Japanese, were saved by the dropping of the atomic bombs to end the war. Sekai no Kokuki.

A Japanese ground crew somewhat reluctantly turn over their Hayate to occupying Americans, August 1945. Koku Fan.

were up against. The Philippines fighting had demonstrated that they needed it.

Help from the Homeland
Exactly the same thing was happening in Japan. The Hayate was being dissected by the Japanese Army, and steps were being taken to enhance mechanical reliability and improve performance. The Hayate was continually being tested, and new ideas were considered in profusion. At the 1st Air Technical Laboratory at Tachikawa a ski-equipped pre-production Hayate was under test in May 1944 for possible use in Manchukuo or the northern Kuriles. Poor performance, reported by test pilot Imamura, a Technical Major on the staff at Fussa, ended the idea.

Engine vibration tests were conducted in August 1944, just as the Hayate entered combat, with mounting modifications incorporated in the production lines. Armament changes were also made, with model variants entering production in parallel with the Ki.84A. With two wing-mounted 20 mm. Ho.5 cannon, and two more on the fuselage, the Hayate became the four-cannon Ki.84B, followed by the

De-fanged "Frank" missing propeller in accordance with Allied occupation instructions signifies the end of the operational Hayate. Sekai no Kokuki.

Late production Ki.84-II Hayate had wooden rear fuselage and wingtips. It was entering regimental service when the war ended. Koku Fan.

Ki.84C with two 20 mm. Ho.5 and two 30 mm. Ho.105 cannon. Known in service as the Type 4 Fighter Model B and Type 4 Fighter Model C respectively, the newer models entered service in the Philippines and Japan before the end of 1944. Plans were even made for a two-seat dual control trainer version for conversion training.

On the Ota Plant floor propellers have been removed to prevent unauthorized removal or use of aircraft. Koku Fan.

None were built, although a number of two-seat versions were created out of existing Ki-84 aircraft in which case the second set of controls was missing.

The most critical problem facing the Hayate was the total unreliability of its power plant. Low oil pressures and high operating temperatures continually caused trouble. The greatest fear of a Hayate pilot was engine overheating. One moment things would be humming, and then suddenly the oil temperature would go up over 85°C as the oil cooler would stop functioning. In five or ten minutes you could see the trouble as a thin stream of black smoke came out of the exhausts. As the Ha-45 heated up

Production at Nakajima's Ota Plant, single-seat one-way Ki.115 Tsurugi suicide bomber at left, Hayates at right. Donald W. Thorpe.

An inconceivable weapons system to Westerners, the Nakajima Ki.115 suicide bomber had lines similar to the combat Ki.84-II at right rear. Koku Fan.

the smoke would turn white, and then thick and black as the engine froze. The sequence took ten to fifteen minutes, and chances were that the pilot was too far away from his base to make it back. It was just like getting shot down, and there wasn't a thing that could be done about it. In combat, if a Hayate was flown upside down, the oil pressure dropped to zero and the engine was sure to freeze. The whole problem was still under investigation at the 1st Air Technical Laboratory at Tachikawa when the war ended.

Fuel pressure drops were also a problem. Later production models mounted the improved Ha.45/ 21, a model that offered slight improvement. It wasn't until the Ha.45/23 was available, with its low-pressure fuel injection system, that the problem was partially solved. Just as the new engine began to reach the Hayate production lines, its own production was all but stopped by an American B-29 attack.

Other Hayate problems were a result of material shortages. Low stocks of dural led to tests of wooden tail surfaces, with production proceeding at Nakajima in the spring of 1945 on the Type 4 Fighter Modified, Model 2, Ki.84-II "Hayate Kai" in which the wing tips, control rods, and much of the

Hayate technology and experience was applied to the Nakajima Ki.87 Army Experimental High Altitude Fighter, an end-of-war interceptor project. William Green.

Power for the Nakajima Ki.87 was the Mitsubishi Ha.44/21 (Ha.219ru), a variation of which was also scheduled for the Ki.117 Hayate Ki.84N intercepter project. Nakajima Hikoki.

rear fuselage were made of wood. Powered by the Ha.45/21, and later the Ha.45/23 and Ha.45/25, the Model 2 Hayates supplemented and would have ultimately replaced the earlier models. A project was initiated to convert some examples of the Hayate into an intercepter fighter in which a fifth 20mm Ho.5 cannon was mounted in the after fuselage, firing upwards at a 45-degree angle through the rear of the cockpit canopy. The purpose was to come in under B-29 bombers and fire upward and pump as many shells in the direction of the American bombers as 300 rounds would permit. It offered an approach to the high flying raiders that might otherwise not be possible to achieve. Examples were completed in September 1944 as the Type 4 Fighter Model D Ki.84D although full production was never authorized, with the Ki.84-II taking its place in the queue line.

The most dramatic attempts at material conservation and utilization were the "Steel Hayate" and "Wooden Hayate" projects. The first to be undertaken was given the Army designation Ki.113 Army Experimental Fighter Hayate in September 1944. The basic idea was to use carbon steel instead of dural for the ribs, bulkheads, forged parts and even the outer skin surfaces. Steel structure tests were

Lines of the Ki.87 prototype serial 8701 were similar to the Ki.84 Hayate. Nakajima Hikoki.

Major airframe design difference of the Ki.87 from the Ki.84 Hayate is the wide outboard landing gear for rough airfields. Nakajima Hikoki.

started under the direction of Technical Captain Fujishina of the 1st Air Technical Laboratory in October 1944, and assemblies were completed in January 1945. First flown in July 1945, the project was dropped even though three more experimental aircraft were being assembled and some 30 more were scheduled for production and evaluation. The high gross weight and poor resulting performance was a critical factor, but the primary decision to forget the idea was based on the fact that existing production facilities at Nakajima's Ota Plant couldn't handle the difficult material.

The Ki.87 high altitude fighter had an exhaust supercharger mounted on its right side. Nakajima Hikoki.

Hayate lines can be made out in the Tachikawa Ki.94-II project, with the aircraft redesignated as the Tachikawa Ki.104 for future development. Sekai no Kokuki.

The wooden Hayate project had a similar fate, although its potential was far greater. First conceived as a possibility by the 1st Air Technical Laboratory staff in the summer of 1944, following a series of studies on the use of wood in aircraft that had been started in March 1943, the JAAF assigned the project to Tachikawa in October 1944 as the Ki.106 Army Experimental Fighter. Long the "second source" for Nakajima-designed fighters, and producer of the Hayabusa ever since it was replaced on the Nakajima production lines, Tachikawa offered a reservoir of fighter productive capacity to the Army. The first task was design, and it was extremely difficult. The demand to re-create the Hayate's lines in wood was almost too much. Wood just couldn't be bent that way, and when it was cut or curved to conform to the Hayate pattern its strength was in question. By the spring of 1945 the Ebetsu shops of the Ohji Paper Company, Ltd., subcontractor to Tachikawa, were busy gluing three examples of the new fighter together. Much of the work was being done by High School girls who just did what they were told, thereby fabricating a fighter even though they were completely unskilled in its production. Tachikawa engineers Shinagawa and Nakagawa, the chief instigators of the project, rushed to Burma when a British DH.98 Mosquito was downed in fair condition so that they could study its construction details. They were pleased with their findings. Impressed with the Mosquito, they still ranked their Ki.106 project higher on the design scale. Production proceeded, and in June 1945 the first example was completed. The aircraft was beautiful, and apart from a few detailed points to adjust

The Tachikawa Ki.94-II project owed a great deal to the Hayate, with both the Nakajima Ki.117 (Ki.84N) high altitude interceptor and the Tachikawa project to be powered by the supercharged Ha.219ru in its Ha.44/12 model. One Ki.94-II was completed but never flown.

for the use of wood, it looked for all the world like a Hayate. One of its most dazzling features was its finish. Sanded and sealed with lacquer like a fine piece of furniture, the plywood skin of the Ki.106 "Wooden Hayate" was then polished after application of a thick coat of wax. Powered with the standard Ha.45/21, and armed with four 20mm. Ho.5 cannon, the prototype was 600 pounds heavier than its parent Ki.84B. Test flown in July, the Ki.106 almost equalled the production Hayate in level speed primarily due to its fantastic lacquered finish. But the weight penalty showed up in other areas. Climb was terrible, and the aircraft had lost the famous Hayate maneuverability. When the second experimental Ki.106 was being finished the armament was

Pressurized cabin capsule of the Tachikawa Ki.94-II, a development that was never attempted with any Hayate project. Sekai no Kokuki.

The first of the captured and revitalized Philippine "Frank" fighters was in the air in a matter of weeks by Technical Air Intelligence Unit S.W.P.A.to learn its secrets. USAAF.

Coded S17, the fixed up Clark Field "Frank" was flown against American fighters in combat evaluation tests on the spot over the Philippines. USAAF.

An elegant aircraft in many ways, maintenance problems with S17 revealed the mechanical weaknesses of the "Frank." USAAF.

reduced to two cannon in hopes of correcting the performance faults by making the aircraft lighter. Undergoing tests in August 1945, flown by Fussa test pilot Major Yasuhiki Kuroe, the first Ki.106 hit 618 km. /hr. at 7,300 metres. At that point the plywood skin began to peel off in the air, but Kuroe landed the aircraft safely. This led to more work on the bonding adhesives, and further tests.

The second Ki.106 incorporated the changes, and was being shipped to Fukuo near Tokyo on 13 August 1945, to await the arrival of Major Kuroe for further testing. The end of the war stopped the plan, and this aircraft was picked up and preserved by the occupying Americans for evaluation of the idea in the United States. The Japanese themselves had all but given up on their plan, coming to the conclusion that mass production of the Ki.106 was impossible as

the required man-hours almost doubled that of the Hayate. Design problems were also not completely solved. For instance, the wing spar, requiring almost impossible bends, kept snapping back to its original position on its jigs. The thought of having that happen in the air was enough to make any Hayate-Kai pilot worry himself to death.

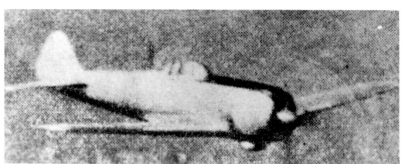

One thing that was learned in a hurry was that with a quick glance in the air "Frank" looked like a stretched and heavier Ki.43 Hayabusa, alerting Allied air crews to be on guard for the new "Oscar" with a bite. USN.

Brought to the United States, "Frank" test model "302" was tested in 1946. The project was soon dropped. Peter M. Bowers.

Another lesson with "Frank." Lack of a fire extinguisher in the Hayate led to a quick installation on "302" for protection during flight tests. USAAF.

Test aircraft 302, front. USAAF.

Other efforts were made to increase Hayate production to assure a steady supply in the face of increasing B-29 attacks on the Homeland. One answer was to displace the production, and by March of 1945 the Ha.45/21 powered Hayate was in production at the Harbin, Manchukuo, plant of the Manshu Aeroplane Manufacturing Company. Other dispersal plants were being set up by Nakajima in caves, tunnels, schools and small factories to keep Hayate production going through the bombings.

It was the Manshu production effort that gave the JAAF another chance at improving the reliability of the Hayate in the air. With engineering time jammed in Japan, the Manshu design group undertook the conversion of the Ki.84 to Mitsubishi Ha.112-II (Ha. 33 /62) Kinsei power. This was a much lower rated engine, but it was also lighter. Taking the fourth Ki.84 off their production line at Harbin, and fitting it with the 1,350 h.p. engine, the satellite nation's engineers were converting the

modified fighter in April 1945. The conversion had already proved itself with the Ki.100 adaptation of the Ki.61-II Hien, and it would do so again with the Manshu Hayate under a hurriedly assigned Army Ki.116 designation. The Manshu staff worked night and day to convert the aircraft, lengthening the engine mount and enlarging the vertical tail to balance the airframe with the lighter engine. A thousand pounds had been cut out of the Hayate design in the process, and Manshu engineers felt they could have cut another 10 per cent if they put their mind to it. Although testing time was limited the Ki.116 performed well, hitting almost 500 m.p.h. and comparing to the Kawasaki Ki.100-Ib. It is probable that the model would have been produced if the war had stretched into 1946.

The Final Fight

While the engineering race continued, the progress of the American and Allied advance escalated. With the collapse of the Philippines the front moved

Abandoned in China, former Japanese Hayate fighters found themselves in Nationalist Chinese service. This Ki.84A is at Nanking, August 1946. David C. Lucabaugh.

closer to Japan. By March 1945 the homeland firebombing raids had begun, and the JAAF was frantic over its inability to defend Japan. The Hayate was little help. With the Ki.84-equipped 22nd, 23rd, 47th, 51st, 52nd and 200th Air Regiments now assigned to the 10th Air Division's Eastern Defense Sector; the 20th, 70th, 111th, 112th and 146th in the 11th Air Division's Central Defense Sector; and the 71st, 101st, 102nd and 103rd in the 12th Air Division's Western Defense Sector; the fighter was numerically important in the defense of Japan. But it was impotent against the B-29. A tactical fighter, the Hayate could be used against escorting Allied fighters or carrier aircraft, but was only rarely successful against the Superfortress. Its real test of strength came elsewhere; over Okinawa, in China and in South-east Asia. With the invasion of Okinawa in April, Hayate units were moved to south-

ern Kyushu for hit-and-run raids on the American positions. They kept it up until the battle was over in June, with Hayates being used in both conventional and special attack suicide missions. Thrown in again at enemy transports in their bombing role, the Hayates were also used in tactical strikes on enemy airfields. On one volunteer mission 11 Hayates suddenly struck the enemy airfields in the

Test aircraft 302, rear. USAAF.

Left at Nanking, China, and pressed into CAF (Chinese Air Force) service, by summer 1946 this Ki.84B or Ki.84C became a mechanical poster for patriotic statements which were painted over the Chinese insignia. Kawasaki Ki.48 "Lily" bomber in background. David C. Lucabaugh.

north and center of Okinawa the night of 15 April 1945, dropping their bombs on the standing American aircraft. The resultant explosions cheered the defending Japanese soldiers on the island although the cost was high. Eight of the Hayates never returned, and a ninth luckily crash landed on the small island of Kikai Jima, with its pilot barely missing death or capture.

In China and Chosen, the Hayate was back in evidence with the 22nd, 25th and 85th Air Regiments. Manchukuo harbored the 70th, elements of the 85th, and 104th Air Regiments, and the 24th Independent Air Company. On Formosa the bypassed 13th, 21st, 24th, 29th and 50th were on hand. To the south, in Indo-China and Thailand, the fighter equipped the 13th and 64th Air Regi-

A tough adversary even though one war was over. Overpainted in Nationalist Chinese markings at Peking (Beijing) when the Pacific War ended, this late model Hayate was re-captured by the Red Army of China and entered their air arm early in 1946. It was flown by Japanese mercenary pilots. It's origin is likely the 104th Fighter Air Regiment of the JAAF stationed in Manchukuo and North China at the time of the Soviet invasion in August 1945. Peter M. Bowers.

Survival of the fittest. "Frank 1" test project "301" survived the scrap heap to be displayed in the United States in the 1950s. Water tank in background says "Osbourne," revealing location to be Patterson Field, Ohio. Town has disappeared, as has Fairfield, Ohio, at Wright Field. Replacement town is a combination of both: Fairborn.

ments. They were the last new fighters to be received by these overseas units. The Hayate pilots were among those that ran up the highest combat scores. Captain Hideshima, killed over Japan, had shot down 44 enemy aircraft from the Sino-Japanese "incident" to the time of his death; Captain Nakazu Ozaki killed over China with the 25th Air Regiment scored 40; Lieutenant Morikichi Kanae, commander of the 25th Air Regiment, survived the war with 25 "kills"; Sergeant Kobayashi, flying Shoki and Hayate fighters with the 47th Regiment in the defence of Tokyo, died after his 12th victory over a B-29; Sergeant Major Goro Miyamoto, flying the Hayate, and later the 5-Sen Ki.100, survived the war with 26 "kills"; in Thailand with the 64th Air Regiment, Warrant Officer Yoshihito Yasuda survived the war with a score of over 30; Corporal Noboru Naito, flying the Ki.84-II with the 520th Temporary Interception Regiment, scored three; Lieu-

tenant Tomiya, with the 104th Air Regiment at Anzan, Manchukuo, had the same score.

The superior characteristics of the Hayate did not go unnoticed, in spite of the aircraft's handicaps. In the closing months of war a number of improvement projects had captured JAAF attention. One of the first, a high-altitude interceptor version of the basic Ki.84 series, made use of a pre-production airframe to which wide-span wings were added. Known as the Ki.84N project, with supercharged Nakajima Ha.219 power of 2,400 h.p., the variant was to be further developed as the Ki.117 following an Army-sponsored design meeting on 4 June 1945. An even longer-span version became the Ki.84P project with a wing area of 24.5 square meters and powered by the 2,450 h.p. Ha. 44/13 radial. In a more conventional mode, the Ki.84R project would make use of the supercharged Ha.45/44 engine with a turbo-supercharger on the under-

The Clark Field S17 lives. The jazzy color scheme is wrong, and the simulated 68th Fighter Air Regiment Ki.61 Hien unit markings are incorrect, but this restored and flyable "Frank" survived in a private museum in the United States for years. It was transferred to Japan where it survives in its restored 11th Fighter Air Regiment markings in the War Museum in Kyoto.

side of the fuselage. The prototype was 80% complete when the war ended. The projected Ki.84-III production model may have been the same aircraft. Other advanced projects, such as the Nakajima Ki.87 and the Tachikawa Ki.94-II and Ki.104 supercharged interceptors, showed obvious Hayate influence.

The end of the Pacific War didn't abruptly end the Hayate's career. While hundreds were found in Japan, and ultimately destroyed in the Allied Occupation's demilitarization program, numerous other examples survived in mainland China where they were taken over by both sides in China's civil war. Examples found in Nanking, Peking (Beijing) and Hankow were quickly marked with Nationalist Chinese insignia, although they do not appear to have been flown in combat. The Chinese Communist forces, however, made some use of the high-performance fighters. Picking up examples in Manchukuo and North China, as well as the Nationalist Hayates at Peking, the Red Army stripped them of their paint and put them into service. Flown by Japanese mercenary pilots, and ultimately by Chinese pilots trained at a Japanese-manned flight school at Harbin, Manchuria, the Hayates were used sporadically on strafing missions in advance of the Communist ground forces. Maintenance and replacement problems soon put them out of commission, and the Hayate ended its days on the ground in helpless peace.

Dark Red-Brown

Indigo anti-glare panel

Natural Metal

Green dapple on Natural Metal

Dark Brown, spinners

A6
Upper surfaces,
standard position of Hinomaru
applicable to all side-views,
see note regarding
presentation of Hinomaru.

Note:
Hinomaru shown black.

A1
Upper surfaces

A1
Under surfaces,
standard position of Hinomaru
applicable to all side-views.

Note: Under surfaces.
Natural Metal
A1, 4
B2, 3, 4, 6
E1, 6
F1, 2, 3, 4, 6
G1, 4
FC2, 3, 4, 5

Very Pale Grey
A2, 3

Pale Grey
A5, 6
B1, 5
C1, 2, 3, 4, 5, 6
D1, 2, 3, 4, 5, 6
E2, 3, 4, 5
F5,
G2, 3, 5, 6
H6
FC1

Pale Blue
H1, 2, 3, 4, 5

B6
Upper surfaces.

Note:
Yellow leading edge
stripe shown black.

B6
Under surfaces.

B2/3
Upper surfaces

Yellow, spinners

Dark Green

Note:
Upper surface Hinomaru
with white ring.
A1, 2, 3, 4, 5, 6
B1, 2, 3, 5,
C1, 2, 3, 4, 5, 6
D1, 2, 3, 4, 5, 6
E2, 3, 4, 6
F1, 2, 4, 5
G2, 3, 5, 6
H6

Yellow, spinners

F3
Under surfaces.
Note: Fuselage panels
from green/grey
camouflaged aircraft.

G5
Under surfaces.
Natural Metal

Dark Green

F3
Upper surfaces.

G5
Upper surfaces.

Pale Grey

E6
Upper surfaces

G4
Upper surfaces.

G4
Under surfaces.

E1
Upper surfaces.

Natural Metal.

G1
Upper surfaces.

Green on
Natural Metal

Black Green

H5
Under surfaces.
Note: No yellow
leading edge.

H5
Upper surfaces.

Natural Metal.

FC5
Upper surfaces,
under surfaces identical.

FC4
Under surfaces.
Note Hinomaru faintly visible.

Pale Blue

H2/3/4
Under surfaces.

FC4
Upper surfaces.
Paint scheme on this aircraft
very weathered.

Indigo, anti-glare panel

Dark Green

H2/3/4
Upper surfaces.

H3
Under surface detail.
Note: blue wheel covers
shown black.

FC2
Upper surfaces.

Dark Brown, spinners.

Green dapple
on Natural Metal

AIR REGIMENTS
Units Operating Ki.84 Type 4 Fighter Hayate

Regiment	When Used	Area of Operations	Former A/C	Later A/C	Comments
1st Fighter	Aug. 1944-July 1945	Philippines. Japan.	Ki.27, Ki.43	None	Saw much combat. Sent to Philippines 22 Sept. 1944 to join 12th Air Brigade, 4th Air Army. Commander was "Ace" Major Saburo Togo (21 kills), with last commander Captain Hedonosake Shishimoto. Disbanded in Japan at Shimodate in July 1945.
2nd Reconnaissance	Jan. 1945-15 July 1945	Japan	Ki.15, Ki.36, Ki.27, Ki.43,	None	Flew Ki.84 in high-speed reconnaissance. Unit officially disbanded 15 July 1945.
11th Fighter	Sept. 1944-end of war	Philippines. Japan.	Ki.27, Ki.43	None	Saw much combat. Sent to Philippines 22 Sept. 1944. Virtually annihilated there. Unit stationed at Clark Field. Flew both Ki.43 and Ki.84 in Philippines. Disbanded at Takahagi, Saitama, Japan at end of war.

Regiment	When Used	Area of Operations	Former A/C	Later A/C	Comments
13th Fighter	Feb. 1945-end of war	Philippines. Syonan (Singapore). French Indo-China. Thailand. Formosa.	Ki.10, Ki.15, Ki.27, Ki.43, Ki.45	None	Unit used five aircraft types during Pacific War. Sent to Celebes in the Southern Philippines and moved north in Dec. 1944 as part of 4th Air Army. Pulled out early in 1945 and moved south. Stationed in Indo-China and Thailand from Feb. 1945 until early August. Disbanded at Heito, South Formosa, at end of war.
20th Fighter	Feb. 1945-end of war	Philippines. Formosa. Okinawa. Japan (Central Defense Sector).	Ki.43	None	Sent to 4th Air Army, Philippines, Nov. 1944. Returned to Formosa in Feb. 1945 to receive Ki.84. Thrown into Okinawa battle. Disbanded at Taichu, Formosa, at end of war.
21st Fighter	May 1944-end of war	Japan. Philippines. Formosa.	Ki.27, Ki.43	Ki.45	Sent to Philippines in summer 1944. First unit to fly Ki.84 in Philippines. Decimated there. Returned to Formosa early in 1945. Disbanded at Toen, Formosa, at end of war.

Regiment	When Used	Area of Operations	Former A/C	Later A/C	Comments
22nd Fighter	5 March 1944-end of war	Japan. China. Philippines. Japan (Eastern Defense Sector). Chosen (Korea).	Ki.44	None	Commanded by Major Iwashi. First combat unit to fly Ki.84, Hankow, China, air defense. Unit one of four to receive Imperial award for distinguished combat performance. Shifted to 12th Air Brigade, 4th Air Army, Philippines on 22 Sept. 1944. Disbanded at Kimpo, Seoul, Chosen (South Korea) at end of war.
23rd Fighter	Spring 1945-end of war	Japan (Eastern Defense Sector)	Ki.43, Ki.44, Ki.61	None	Ki.43 unit returned from Iwo Jima and reorganized as home defense unit formed at Ota Airfield, Inba, Chiba on 11 Oct. 1944. Flew mixed bag of Ki.43, Ki.44, Ki.61 with a few Ki.84 later assigned. Both training and combat. Disbanded at Inba, Chiba, at end of war.

Regiment	When Used	Area of Operations	Former A/C	Later A/C	Comments
24th Fighter	March 1945-end of war	Japan. Okinawa. Formosa.	Ki.27, Ki.43	Ki.45	One of JAAF "Old Units" flying Ki.43 in Philippines. Pulled out early in 1945 and re-equipped with Ki.84 for Okinawa campaign. Saw much combat. Finally reassigned to Formosa and disbanded there at Taito at end of war.
25th Fighter	March 1945-end of war	China. Chosen (Korea)	Ki.43	Ki.100	Chinese occupation force. Fought against Chinese Air Force which later acquired and used its aircraft. Flew both Ki.84 and Ki.100 in closing months of war. Disbanded at Suigen, Chosen (Korea) at end of war.
29th Fighter	Nov. 1944-end of war	Philippines. Japan. Formosa.	Ki.44	None	Sent to Philippines reaching 4th Air Army in November 1944. Formerly 29th Independent Air Company. Unit disbanded at Taichu, Formosa, at end of war.
47th Fighter	24 Dec. 1943-end of war	Japan, Okinawa, Japan (Eastern Defense Sector)	Ki.43, Ki.44	None	Formerly 47th Independent Air Company. Known as "Kingfisher Regiment" based on previous assignment. Disbanded at Ozuki, Yamaguchi.

Regiment	When Used	Area of Operations	Former A/C	Later A/C	Comments
50th Fighter	Nov. 1944-end of war	Burma. Thailand. French Indo-China. Philippines. Formosa	Ki.27, Ki.43, Ki.44	None	Crack "Overseas" unit. Occupation force in French Indo-China and Thailand. Moved north to Formosa in spring 1945 and conversion to Ki.84. Unit disbanded at Kagi, Formosa, at end of war.
51st Fighter	June 1944-end of war	Japan. Philippines. Japan (Home Island Defense)	Ki.43	None	Unit sent to Philippines 22 Sept. 1944 to join 16th Air Brigade, 4th Air Army. Commander was Major Tadao Ikeda. Unit disbanded at Shimodate, Ibaraki, Japan, at end of war.
52nd Fighter	June 1944-end of war	Japan. Philippines. Okinawa. Japan (Eastern Defense Sector)	Ki.43	None	Unit sent to Philippines 22 Sept. 1944 to join 16th Air Brigade, 4th Air Army. Commander was Major Ikida Takano. Unit disbanded at Chofu, Tokyo, Japan, at end of war.
64th Fighter	Summer 1945-end of war	Thailand	Ki.10, Ki.27, Ki.43, P-40, Ki.44	None	Brief use of the Ki.44 on an exploratory basis prior to conversion to Ki.84. Converted to Ki.84 in Thailand as the war ended. Retained name as "Kato Regiment." Disbanded at Kuracoul in SE Asia at end of war.

Regiment	When Used	Area of Operations	Former A/C	Later A/C	Comments
70th Fighter	30 July 1944-end of war	Japan (Central Defense Sector). Manchukuo.	Ki.27, Ki.44, Ki.45	Ki.45	Home island defense unit assigned to Tokyo air defense after Doolittle Raid in April 1941. Primary fighter in 1944 to end of war was Ki.44 with Ki.84 added after unit re-training at Akeno in July 1944. Commander was Major Tokuyuki Sakato. Disbanded at Matsudo, Chiba, Japan, at end of war.
71st Fighter	30 June 1944-end of war	Japan. Philippines. Japan (Western Defense Sector)	Ki.43, Ki.44	None	Hastily formed Fighter Air Regiment for Philippines defense. Formerly light bomber unit reformed in Japan 30 June 1944. Flew Ki.43 and Ki.84 in the Philippines. Disbanded at Hofu, Yamaguchi, Japan, at end of war.

Regiment	When Used	Area of Operations	Former A/C	Later A/C	Comments
72nd Fighter	30 June 1944	Japan. Philippines.	Ki.43	None	Hastily formed Fighter Air Regiment for Philippines defense. Formed in Japan 30 June 1944. Commander was Major Eisuke Tsusake. Arrived in Philippines in Dec. 1944 and assigned to 4th Air Army. Unit annihilated. Officially disbanded for the records on 30 May 1945.
73rd Fighter	June 1944-30 May 1945	Japan. Philippines.	Ki.43	None	Established Ki.43 unit equipped with Ki.84 and sent to Philippines in Dec. 1944. Commander was Major Teruo Misumi. Unit virtually annihilated in Philippines. Officially disbanded for the records on 30 May 1945.
85th Fighter	Sept. 1944-end of war	China. Chosen. Manchukuo.	Ki.27, Ki.44	None	Nanking, China, air defense and China occupation force. Shifted to Chosen (Korea) in spring 1945. Commander was Major Togo Saito. Unit disbanded at Seoul, Chosen (South Korea) at end of war.

Regiment	When Used	Area of Operations	Former A/C	Later A/C	Comments
101st Fighter	10 Nov. 1944-end of war	Okinawa. Japan (Home Island Defense).	Ki.43	None	Home Island Defense unit formed at Kameyama, Shimane, Japan, 10 Nov. 1944. Commander was Major Mitake Sakamoto. Flew Ki.43 and Ki.84. Disbanded at Takamatsu, Kagawa, Japan, at end of war.
102nd Fighter	10 Nov. 1944- 30 July 1945	Okinawa. Japan (Home Island Defense).	Ki.43	None	Companion regiment to 101st formed at Kameyama, Shimane, Japan, 10 Nov. 1944. Unit officially disbanded 30 July 1945 due to losses with remains transferred to 103rd Fighter Air Regiment.
103rd Fighter	Sept. 1944-end of war	Yura, Awaji Islands.	Ki.43	None	Advance island defense for Home Islands. Unit formed at Kameyama, Shimane, Japan, 25 Aug. 1944. Later expanded by remnants of 102nd Air Regiment. Disbanded at Yura ("Japanese Southern Islands") at end of war.

Regiment	When Used	Area of Operations	Former A/C	Later A/C	Comments
104th Fighter	30 Nov. 1944-end of war	Manchukuo	Ki.43, Ki.44	None	Counter Soviet Patrol. Crack Ki.84 regiment remaining in Manchukuo. Unit formed at Heizan, Manchukuo, 30 Nov. 1944. Commander was Major Yosuke Okazaki. Fought against Soviet and Mongolian aircraft in "7 Day War." Disbanded at Anzan, Manchukuo, at end of war.
111th Fighter	10 July 1945-end of war	Japan (Central Defense Sector).	None	Ki.100	One of the last JAAF units to be created. Flew both Ki.84 and Ki.100. Last unit to be formed at Akeno, going active the same day Akeno was closed. Commander was Lieut. Colonel Tadashi Ishikawa. Unit disbanded at Komaki, Gifu. Japan, at end of war.
112th Fighter	10 July 1945-end of war	Japan (Central Defense Sector).	Ki.43	Ki.100	One of the last JAAF regiments to be created. Unit formed at Komaki, Gifu, Japan, 10 July 1945 flying mixed bag of Ki.43, Ki.84, Ki.100. Commander was Lieut. Colonel Hedemi. Disbanded after the war at Gifu.

Regiment	When Used	Area of Operations	Former A/C	Later A/C	Comments
200th Fighter	12 Oct. 1944-30 May 1945	Philippines. Japan (Home Island Defense).	None	Ki.100	Unit formed at Akeno, Mie, Japan, 12 Oct. 1944 with Ki.84 as original equipment. Sent to 4th Air Army in Philippines. Decimated there. Officially disbanded for the records 30 May 1945.
246th Fighter	Autumn 1944-end of war	Philippines. Japan (Central Defense Sector).	Ki.27, Ki.43, Ki.44	None	Established home island defense unit received Ki.44 in July 1943. Ki.84 introduced to unit and shipped to 4th Air Army in Philippines in Nov. 1944. Returned to Osaka defense in April 1945. Commander was Major Ishikawa. Disbanded at Taisho, Osaka, Japan, end of war.
520th Temporary Interception	Dec. 1944-March 1945	Japan (Home Island Defense).	None	None	Hastily formed air defense unit with pilots and aircraft later reassigned to other units. Based at Nakatsu Airfield between Dec. 1944 and March 1945. One of few units to operate Ki.84-II.

INDEPENDENT AIR COMPANIES

Company	When Used	Area of Operations	Former A/C	Later A/C	Comments
24th Fighter	Jan. 1945-30 May 1945	Philippines. Sumatra. Formosa.	Ki.43	None	One of the few Ki.84 overseas units other than in China or Philippines. Unit arrived in Philippines Oct. 1944. Transferred to Sumatra and Formosa in early 1945. Decimated in special attack missions and disbanded for the records 30 May 1945.
Experimental Service Evaluation	Oct. 1943-March 1944	Japan.	None	None	Service evaluation of pre-production Ki.84 under operational conditions. Unit disbanded March 1944 with personnel and aircraft transferring to 22nd Air Regiment to go to China and later Philippines.

FLIGHT TRAINING UNITS

Company	When Used	Area of Operations	Former A/C	Later A/C	Comments
1st	22 July 1944-end of war	Japan	Ki.43	None	Unit formed 22 July 1944 with Ki.43 as original equipment, augmented by Ki.84. Disbanded at end of war.
8th	31 May 1944-end of war	Japan	None	None	First Flight Training Unit to fly Ki.84. Unit formed 31 May 1944 and disbanded at end of war.
10th	30 Nov. 1944-end of war	Japan	None	None	Last Flight Training Unit to be formed. Doubled in Home Defense duties. Formed 30 Nov. 1944 and disbanded at end of war.
13th	15 Sept. 1944-end of war	Japan	Ki.43	None	Flew both Ki.43 and Ki.84 when formed 15 Sept. 1944. Disbanded at end of war.
14th	Oct. 1944-31 Dec. 1944	Japan	Ki.43	None	Short-lived unit formed in Oct. 1944 and flying both Ki.43 and Ki.84. Disbanded two months later.

TRAINING SCHOOLS

School	When Used	Area of Operations	Former A/C	Later A/C	Comments
Akeno Army Flying School	Feb. 1944-10 June 1944	Akeno, Hitachi, Japan	Ki.10, Ki.27, Ki.43, Ki.44, Ki.61, Ki.45	None	First flying school to conduct Ki.84 training. Trained 22nd Air Regiment in Feb. and March 1944 to be first Ki.84 combat unit. Reformed in June 1944 into the Akeno Training Air Division (TAD) with the branch becoming the Hitachi Training Air Division.
Akeno Training Air Division (TAD)	20 June 1944-10 July 1945	Akeno, Japan	Ki.43, Ki.44, Ki.45, Ki.61	Ki.100	Former Akeno Army Flying School. Day fighter combat unit formed in June 1944 with Ki.43 and Ki.44. Also known as Akeno Instructing Flight Division. Formed 111th Air Regiment in July 1945 with unit going active 10 July. School terminated activity same day.
Hokota Training Air Division (TAD)	20 June 1944-10 July 1945	Hokota, Japan	Ki.48, Ki.51, Ki.54	Ki.45	Former light bomber training school pressed into fighter training for home island defense requirements. Also known as Hokota Instructing Flight Division.

Regiment	When Used	Area of Operations	Former A/C	Later A/C	Comments
Army Aviation Maintenance School	Summer 1944-end of war	Tokorozawa, Japan	All current JAAF aircraft	All current JAAF aircraft	Army Aviation Maintenance School for Ki.84 maintenance and crew repair training.
Tachikawa Instructing Maintenance Division	Autumn 1944-end of war	Tachikawa, Japan	All current JAAF aircraft	All current JAAF aircraft	Maintenance and repair training for Philippines and Home Island Defense units.

RAMMING ATTACK UNITS (Taiatari)

Regiment	When Used	Area of Operations	Former A/C	Later A/C	Comments
(57th) Shinten Seiku-Tai	Summer 1945-end of war	Japan (Home Island Defense)	None	None	Formed within the 57th Air Regiment defending Tokyo as one of the few air-to-air Taiatari (Body Crashing) suicide B-29 ramming attacks. Pilots and missions selected on a volunteer basis.

FOREIGN SERVICE

Country and Unit	When Used	Area of Operations	Comments
Republic of China (Nationalist China)	1945-1948	China	Captured examples of former JAAF 85th and 104th Air Regiments picked up in China and Manchuria. A few examples flown by the Nationalists in Chinese Civil War 1946-1949. Prime purpose was to hold in reserve in event American aid was cut and fighters were needed.
Red Army Air Force (Communist China)	Oct. 1945-July 1946	Manchuria, North China, Central China	Former JAAF aircraft acquired in Manchuria and captured from the Chinese Nationalists. Actively flown by Red Army Air Force by Japanese pilots and mentioned in Nationalist Chinese field reports. One of Communist China's first fighters.

Country and Unit	When Used	Area of Operations	Comments
People's Liberation Army Air Force (PLAAF)	July 1946-1949	North China, Central China, Manchuria	The People's Liberation Army Air Force (PLAAF) was formed by the new People's Republic of China in July 1946 out of the earlier Red Army Air Force in China. Sporadic use of the Ki.84 along with the Ki.43, Ki.44 and Ki.61, 1946-1949. Remained in service until replaced by Soviet fighters in 1950.

Note: These lists are not to be regarded as complete as only those units for which Ki.84 use has been confirmed have been identified.

SPECIFICATIONS: Nakajima Ki.84 Type 4 Fighter Hayate (Hurricane)

Note: All dimensions in original Japanese metric. Dimensions and climb in meters (m.), weights in kilograms (kg.), distances in kilometers (km.) and speeds in kilometers per hour (km./hr.). Data in parenthesis are estimates or approximate.

Model and Specs:	Ki.84 Exper.	Ki.84 Exper. Eval	Ki.84 Pre-prod.	Ki.84A	Ki.84B	Ki.84C	Ki.84 Trainer
Span (m.)	11.238	11.238	11.238***	11.238	11.238	11.238	11.238
Length (m.)	—	—	—	9.920	9.920	9.920	9.920
Height (m.)	—	—	—	3.385	3.385	3.385	3.385
Wing Area (m.2)	—	—	—	21.00	21.00	21.00	21.00
Weight Empty (kg.)	—	—	—	2,698	2,698	2,698	—
Weight Loaded (kg.)	—	—	—	3,890	3,750	3,890	—
Weight Loaded Max. (kg.)	—	—	—	—	—	—	—
Max. Speed (km./hr.)	—	624/6,500	—	624/6,000	624/6,500	—	—
Cruising Speed (km./hr.)	—	—	—	624/4,500	—	—	—
Climb (m./min.)	—	5,000/6'26"	—	5,000/5'54"	5,000/6'26"	—	—
Armament- M.G. (mm.)	2x12.7	2x12.7	2x12.7	2x12.7	—	—	None
Armament- Cannon (mm.)	2x20	2x20	2x20	2x20	4x20	2x30, 2x20	None
Armament- Bombs (kg.)	—	—	2x250	2x250	2x250	2x250	None
Power-Mfr.	Nakajima	Nakajima	Nakajima	Nakajima	Nakajima	Nakajima	Nakajima
Type	Ha.45/11	Ha.45/11	Ha.45/11	Ha.45/11†	Ha.45/21	Ha.45/21	Ha.45/21
H.P.	1,800	1,800	1,800	1,800	1,990	1,990	1,990
Crew	1	1	1	1	1	1	2
Aircraft-Mfr.	Nakajima	Nakajima	Nakajima	Nakajima, Manshu	Nakajima	Nakajima	Nakajima
First Built	March 1943	Aug. 1943	March 1944	April 1944	1944	1945	Autumn 1944
Number Built	4*	83**	42	3,450††	(600)	(350)	(20)†††

* First three have single exhaust stack.
** Some examples had racks for 2 x 250 kg. bombs. One example had ski gear.
*** Some examples had increased span to test Ki.117 and Ki.84P design concepts.

† Later models had Ha.45/12, Ha.45/21 and Ha.45/23.
†† All production models A, B and C. Manshu produced 95.
††† Two-seat conversions sans armament. Dual control production model planned.

§ Turbosupercharger.
§§ Included in Ki.84B and Ki.84C production.
§§§ Later models had 2x12.7 and 2x20.
§§§§ Project dropped in favor of Ki.84R.

Ki.84-II	Ki.84D	Ki.84-III	Ki.84P	Ki.84R	Ki.106 "Wooden Hayate"	Ki.113 "Steel Hayate"	Ki.116	Ki.117
11,238	11.238	11.238	—	11.238	11.230	11.238	11.238	—
9.920	9.920	9.920	9.920	9.920	9.950	9.920	—	9.920
3.385	3.385	3.385	3.385	3.385	3.590	3.385	—	3.385
21.00	21.00	21.00	24.50	21.00	21.00	21.50	21.00	22.50
—	—	—	—	—	2,948	2,880	2,300	—
—	—	—	—	—	3,900	3,950	3,500	—
—	—	—	—	—	—	—	—	—
—	—	—	—	—	620/8,000	620/6,500	—	—
—	—	—	—	—	500/6,400	—	—	—
—	—	—	—	—	5,000/5'00"	5,000/6'54"	—	—
—	—	—	2x12.7	2x12.7	None	2x12.7	2x12.7	2x12.7
4x20 or 2x20,2x30	5x20	—	2x20	2x20	4x20§§§	2x20	2x20	2x20
2x250	None	—	—	—	2x250	2x250	—	—
Nakajima	Nakajima	Nakajima	Nakajima	Nakajima	Nakajima	Nakajima	Nakajima	Mitsubishi Nakajima
Ha.45/21	Ha.45/21	Ha.45ru§	Ha.44/13 (Ha.219)	Ha.45/44§	Ha.45/21	Ha.45/21	Ha.33/62 (Ha.112-II)	Ha.44/13 (Ha.219)
2,000	1,990	2,000	2,500	2,000	1,990	1,990	1,500	2,500
1	1	1	1	1	1	1	1	1
Nakajima	Nakajima	Nakajima	Nakajima	Nakajima	Tachikawa	Nakajima	Manshu	Nakajima
1945	Sep. 1944	(Late 1945)	(Late 1945)	(Late 1945)	June 1945	July 1945	April 1945	(Late 1945)
—§§	—	None	None§§§§	None	4	4	1	None

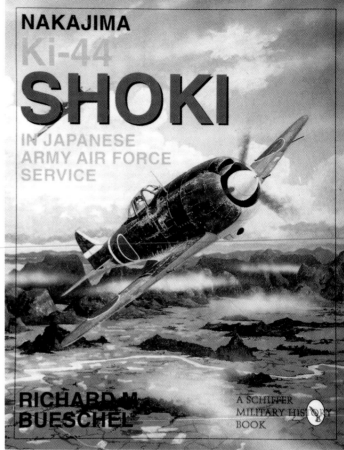

Kawasaki Ki-61 HIEN
In Japanese Army Air Force Service

Richard M. Bueschel

Reknowned Japanese aircraft historian Richard Bueschel revises and updates his classic series of books on Japanese Naval and Army Air Force aircraft of World War II. The JAAF Kawasaki Ki-61 HIEN (Tony) is presented in this volume. All variations and markings are covered in this the fourth in a projected multi-volume series. Others volumes include the *Mitsubishi A6M-1/2/-2N ZERO-SEN*, *Nakajima Ki-43 HAYABUSA*, and *Nakajima Ki-44 SHOKI* (all available from Schiffer Publishing Ltd.).

Size: 8 1/2" x 11" over 100 b/w photographs
64 pages, soft cover
ISBN: 0-7643-0069-5 $14.95
Available September

Nakajima Ki-44 SHOKI
In Japanese Army Air Force Service

Richard M. Bueschel

All variations and markings are covered in this the third book in a multi-volume series.

Size: 8 1/2" x 11" over 100 b/w photographs
64 pages, soft cover
ISBN: 0-88740-914-8 $14.95